HERRING HEYDAY

C000072367

A Portrait of the East Anglian Fishing Industry

by

K. W. Kent

S. B. Publications
1992

Dedicated to my wife, Ethel

Published in 1992 by S.B. Publications.
c/o 19 Grove Road, Seaford, East Sussex BN25 1TP.

Reprinted 1995

ISBN 1 85770 009 0

Typeset and printed by Geo. R. Reeve Ltd., Wymondham, Norfolk NR18 0BD.

CONTENTS

Front cover: Scottish drifters at rest, c.1920s   *Title page:* Steam drifter *Wydale*, YH 105

HERRING SEASON AT GREAT YARMOUTH, c.1953

INTRODUCTION

Many books have been written about some of the larger fishing companies such as the Smiths Dock Trust company and Bloomfields Limited. This book begins with a general view of the East Anglian herring fisheries which took place in Great Yarmouth and Lowestoft each autumn, between early October and the end of November. In the next chapter, I have given a brief account of the Prunier Herring Trophy. This was the prize for which Scottish and English drifters competed annually. The last chapter is devoted to one of the best and most established names to be associated with the fishing industry at Great Yarmouth — the Eastick family.

Over the years, Great Yarmouth was known as the premier fishing port in East Anglia. The town was built up from the holiday trade in the summer and the herring season in the autumn. Many Scottish men and women, from such places as Wick, Methil, Inverness, Buckie, Banff, Fraserburgh, Peterhead, Aberdeen, Lerwick in the Shetlands and Stornoway on the Isle of Lewis, would travel to Great Yarmouth and Lowestoft on special trains for the start of the autumn herring season. The men would work as buyers, salesmen, coopers or other types of shore worker. The women — or Scottish girls, as they were called — gutted and packed the herrings. The fisheries also employed local men and women from Great Yarmouth, Caister, Gorleston, Winterton and from other villages north of Great Yarmouth. Many of the fishermen on the local drifters also came from these places.

K. W. KENT
Gorleston-on-Sea

PORT DISTINGUISHING LETTERS

A	Aberdeen	INS	Inverness
BF	Banff	KY	Kirkcaldy
BK	Berwick	LT	Lowestoft
FR	Fraserburgh	WY	Whitby
GY	Grimsby	YH	Yarmouth
H	Hull		

ABBREVIATIONS USED IN TEXT

M.D.	Motor Drifter	S.D.	Steam Drifter
M.T.	Motor Trawler	S.T.	Steam Trawler
M.D.T.	Motor Drifter/ Trawler	S.D.T.	Steam Drifter/ Trawler
M.C.	Motor Cruiser	S.V.	Sailing Smack
c.	circa	S.Y.	Sailing Yacht

SCOTTISH DRIFTERS ENTERING YARMOUTH HARBOUR, c.1920

A crowd of people watch as the Scottish steam drifter fleet enters the harbour at Great Yarmouth. These drifters worked their way south, reaching Great Yarmouth and Lowestoft in early October. There, they would be joined by drifters from Leith and other English ports such as Berwick, North Shields, Whitby, Hull and Grimsby.

M. V. ROSEDENE, c.1950

The *Rosedene* is seen arriving at Great Yarmouth, heavily laden with empty barrels from Scotland.

THE AUTUMN AND WINTER HERRING GROUNDS.

In late September, the drifters would fish the Dowsing ground. The traditional fishing ground for the October herring was known as the "Smith's Knoll", which is about 45 miles north east of Great Yarmouth. After October, the drifters would go south to fish the Sandettie ground near the Dover Straits. They would also fish the waters off Cap Gris Nez.

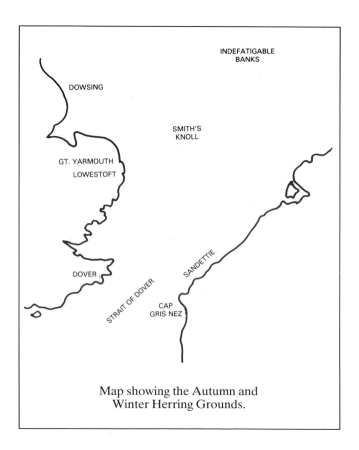

Map showing the Autumn and Winter Herring Grounds.

3

Trawlers in Harbour, Lowestoft

TRAWLERS IN HARBOUR, LOWESTOFT, c.1920

Although the caption on this postcard states that these are trawlers, they are all steam drifters, laid up for the winter in Hamilton Dock. The first steam drifter to be built at Lowestoft was the *Consolation*, LT718, which was constructed in 1897, by Chambers & Colbys yard, for George Catchpole of Kessingland. The cost for a fully equipped drifter would be about £2,000, and these were of wood and, later, steel construction: to quote skipper-owner Ronnie Balls — "the loveliest ship, for the job that was ever built". Between 1900 and 1914, 1,800 drifters were built: they were 70-75ft. in length, had a crew of 10 men and would carry a fleet of 80 to 90 nets.

S. D. *MERBREEZE*, LT365, c.1950

In later years, the drifters were larger. This vessel was built in 1932, by Richards Ironworks Ltd., of Lowestoft. It was registered as LT253, later to be LT365. She was owned by Mr C H J Eastick. In 1939, she had been requisitioned for use as a minesweeper and returned in 1946. A modern drifter/trawler, built in 1959, was 97ft. long and enabled them to carry more fish and a larger fleet of nets — about 100.

"SUNDAY REST", Autumn, 1955

The English drifters would go to sea on Sunday mornings and fish for six nights, landing each day if they had a good catch; they would then have the Saturday night ashore. The Scottish drifters, whose crews were religious people, would not fish on a Sunday. They would go to sea on Monday mornings and fish for five nights — again, landing each day if necessary. The picture shows Scottish motor drifters at Great Yarmouth. On Sundays, there was always a lot of visitors walking from Haven Bridge along the quay looking at the drifters which were berthed three or four abreast on both sides of the river; those near the Fish Wharf were berthed stem to the quay.

RANSACKERS AT WORK, c.1940

For a successful season it was essential that the nets be in good repair. These men are "ransackers" whose job it was to check over drift-nets for damage. They were photographed in a Yarmouth net store. Each net was 35 yards long and 10 yards deep and, to keep the net up, there were about 70 corks fixed to it.

BEATSTERS AT WORK, c.1922

These ladies are "beatsters" whose job was to repair any damaged nets that were found by the ransackers. This picture was also taken in a Yarmouth net store.

SORTING NETS ON DRIFTERS, LOWESTOFT, c.1960

These men are busy stowing the nets in to the hold of one of the modern motor drifters at Lowestoft. The vessel in the background is the *Lizzie West*, LT495, which was the last steam drifter to work from Lowestoft.

A TOW TO SEA, c.1905

Three Lowestoft sailing smacks are being towed out to sea by a paddle tug. In the days of sail, the English boats used for herring drifting were Yarmouth luggers and sailing drifters, all of wooden construction. The Scottish boats were either "fifies", which had a straight stem and straight stern, or "zulues", which had a straight stem and a raked stern. All the boats had to be towed in and out of the harbour, five or six at a time, by steam paddle tugs employed for the job.

TOWING TO SEA, YARMOUTH, c.1905

Another interesting group, this one shows the steam paddle tug *Reaper* towing the sailing smacks *Nell,* YH868, *Orient,* YH1053, and *Primrose,* LT87, out to sea. On the left of the picture is the iron-built, 24 h.p. screw, steam trawler *Sweetheart,* built at Barking in 1885.

SHOT NETS IN THE NAME OF THE LORD, October, 1948

The fishermen are shooting the nets from the Yarmouth steam drifter *Phyllis Mary,* YH578. In the early days, before they had any sophisticated fish-finding equipment like echo-sounders, the fishermen could tell where the herring were by the colour of the water, the diving gannets or the whales — or blowers as they were called. The herring would be on the bottom of the seabed all day and would rise to the surface just before the close (dusk) — that would be the time for the drifter to shoot his nets and hope the herring would swim into them.

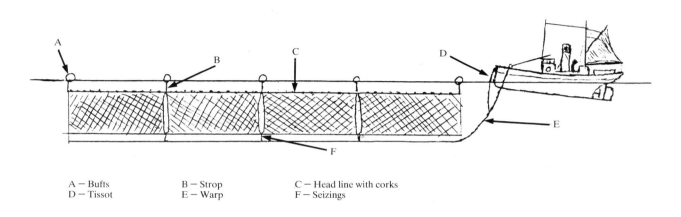

A — Bufts   B — Strop   C — Head line with corks
D — Tissot   E — Warp   F — Seizings

SKETCH OF DRIFTER AND HERRING NETS

The nets were fastened to a warp by seizings; this would keep the net down, like a wall. To keep the top of the net up there were corks along the top which was fastened to buffs (large canvas or plastic buoys) by strops, one buff on each end of the net. The warp was fastened to the tissot, a strong rope that took the strain of the fleet of nets, the other end being attached to the drifter. As the boats could carry a fleet of 80 to 90 nets, this would make a string of nets approximately 2 miles long. The only boats to use the drift net today are the small longshore ones working along the North Norfolk coast, about a mile off shore.

HAULING THE NETS, October, 1948

110 crans of herring are being hauled on to the Yarmouth steam drifter *Phyllis Mary,* built in 1917 and owned by G. Newson & Son Ltd. Today, the modern purseiners, which have replaced the drifters in Scotland, can catch as much herring in one haul as 100 drifters would catch in a week. When the drifters fished the Sandettie and Cap Gris Nez grounds, they would sometimes land their catch at Dover rather than steam all the way back to East Anglia.

14

A RACE FOR THE MARKET, YARMOUTH, c.1922

The people in the foreground are watching these Scottish drifters race to get the best prices for their catches! Great Yarmouth and Lowestoft have had some good and some very bad seasons. The best seasons were from 1899 until 1914. From the late 1920s until the outbreak of World War 2, things were very bad and they lost the market for herring. Sometimes, drifters would come in after 8 or 9 hours hauling and would have to go back to sea and dump their catch.

A SWILL CART, GREAT YARMOUTH, 1956

Swill carts were used to take the empty swills to the drifters for unloading their catches. The swill is a wicker basket, only used at Great Yarmouth. The herrings would be swung ashore from the boats, in $\frac{1}{4}$ cran baskets, and would then be tipped into the swills. The full swills would be taken by horse or motor lorry to the curing yards, factories or fish houses (buildings in which the herring are smoked for kippers, red herring, bloaters or bucklings).

THE CRAN MEASURE

In 1908, the cran became the standard measure for herring. It was $37\frac{1}{2}$ gallons or 28 stones by weight and consisted of approximately 1,320 herring, depending on size. The picture shows the official cran measure in the Maritime Museum at the Sparrow's Nest, Lowestoft. It is said to have been used only once in a dispute on the Lowestoft Market.

120,000 HERRINGS IN HOLD. Nr. GORLESTON

Unloading the herring from the drifters was a laborious job before the cran came into use. They were counted out by hand as follows:

"Warp"=4 herrings
"Long hundred of herring"=33 warps or 132 herrings
"Ten hundred herring"=1,320 herrings

UNLOADING HERRING, GREAT YARMOUTH.

UNLOADING HERRING, GREAT YARMOUTH, c.1910

The herrings are placed in the baskets before being swung ashore. The drifters would carry wooden trunks or, in more modern boats, aluminium trunks, so that they could ice any small catches at sea rather than return straight to port with them.

UNLOADING THE CATCH, THE FISHWHARF, YARMOUTH, c.1921

When filled, the $\frac{1}{4}$ cran baskets are swung ashore to be emptied into the swills. When I was "running out" — carrying the $\frac{1}{4}$ cran baskets and tipping the herring into the swills — we would put one $\frac{1}{4}$ cran into one swill, then one $\frac{1}{4}$ cran in another, then one $\frac{1}{4}$ cran between the two and, finally, one $\frac{1}{4}$ cran in a swill across the two. This was done for easy counting.

UNLOADING THE CATCH, YARMOUTH QUAY, c.1907

This earlier view shows a very busy scene. It seems that unloading was almost finished and, with all those full swills, that it was a good catch. It has been said that, sometimes, it was possible to walk across the river on drifters — that was in the days when there was no control of the shipping in the harbour. Drifters would be landing their catches on both sides of the river, others would be coming in to land, whilst others would be in a hurry to get to sea. With such frantic comings and goings, the harbour would become blocked! There hardly seems to be room for any more in this view!

A MORNING CATCH OF HERRING, LOWESTOFT, c.1903

These men are knee-deep in a large catch of herring! The fish were sold by auction. In the early days, they were sold by the "last" — which was about 13,200 herrings. From 1908, the cran was adopted as the standard measure. (See page 17).

A BUSY CORNER OF HERRING MARKET, LOWESTOFT

A BUSY CORNER OF THE HERRING MARKET, LOWESTOFT, c.1920

Some of the herrings are sold to the home market and large quantities used to be sent by rail to Billingsgate Fish Market in London. Herring were also bought for the kippering trade, canning factories and, more recently, the frozen food factories. A lot of fish were also exported.

KIPPERING HERRING, GT. YARMOUTH.

KIPPERING HERRING, GREAT YARMOUTH, c.1920
These Scottish girls are splitting the herrings for kippers. The girl on the right is holding a line of fish ready for smoking.

GUTTING HERRING, GORLESTON, c.1920

Herrings for export were first lightly salted and then tipped into a farlane — a wooden trough. They were then ready for the girls to gut them. This photograph shows the women gutting fish at a Gorleston Curing Yard — there were yards all along Riverside Road. The curing yards at Great Yarmouth were on the South Denes, where the power station now stands, and on the land of the former Birds Eye factory — in fact, all around that area. At Lowestoft, the yards were on the North Denes, off Whapload Road.

SCOTCH GIRLS GUTTING HERRINGS, LOWESTOFT

SCOTTISH GIRLS GUTTING HERRING, LOWESTOFT, c.1920

The jobs of gutting, pickling and packing the herrings were mostly carried out by Scottish girls who used to follow the herring season down the East Coast. They would work for a week or so at each port — Lowestoft being the most southerly port.

GUTTING HERRING AT THE FARLANES, GORLESTON, c.1920

This close-up view clearly shows what a messy job these girls did. It must have been a cold job too, as the season was in October and November. Except for their bare forearms, most of the girls are well wrapped up.

SCOTTISH GIRL, 58.
N. GORLESTON.

**PACKING THE HERRING,
GORLESTON, c.1920**

After gutting, the fish were packed in barrels.
The white stuff on the lids in the foreground
would be salt as the herring were packed in
brine.

HERRING PACKING, GORLESTON, c.1920

The Scottish girls are packing the herring into the barrels. The man in the foreground is the cooper who would put the lids on. The enormity of the task can be seen from the long lines of barrels that surround this group of workers.

THE CURING YARDS, YARMOUTH, c.1905

The curing yards are seen here looking south, from Main Cross Road. Below are some interesting figures to show the size of the fleet and herring landed:

Year:	Number of drifters prosecuting the fishing:	Crans landed:	Cured herring exported:
1913	1,006	824,213	829,527 barrels
1919	850	453,571	------------------------------
1920	973	616,806	476,000 barrels
1921	872	358,573	590,000 barrels
1922	848	342,237	285,239 barrels

HERRING EXPORT WHARF, GREAT YARMOUTH.

HERRING EXPORT WHARF, GREAT YARMOUTH, c.1910

Herring packing was one of the greatest industries of East Anglia. The barrels of herring were exported to Germany, Poland, Russia and many other European countries. Another export market was the Klondykers and Freshers.

HERRINGS FOR EXPORT, YARMOUTH, October 1948

A consignment of 3,500,000 herrings is being loaded into the motor ship *Gowie,* bound for Germany. The fish here are packed in crates with chipped ice.

HERRINGS FOR EXPORT, GORLESTON, c.1950

The S.S. *Krakow* is waiting to be loaded with barrels of cured herring. After World War 2, the East Anglian herring fishing industry improved after the lean years of the 1930s. There was a small fleet of drifters and a good market. The old steam drifters were replaced by modern diesel drifters. The last drifters to fish from Great Yarmouth were *Strathbeg,* FR202, *Brighter Hope,* FR371, *Girl Marlene,* FR106, and *Golden Gain,* FR59, and these fished for the last time in 1970. Since then, Scottish pair trawlers have landed herring.

33

DE GAUSSING VESSEL *OCEAN PIONEER*

During both World Wars, many of the steam drifters were requisitioned by the Royal Navy and they were employed on the following duties: balloon barrage vessels, De Gaussing vessels, harbour service, hospital ships, torpedo recovery vessels, flare drifters, water carriers, store carriers, auxiliary patrol, damlayers, tenders and antisubmarine. They all did a gallant job for the country, both at home and overseas. In World War 2, the Admiralty had some motor fishing vessels built and, after the war, many of these were sold out of service — many being bought by the Scottish fishermen to replace their old steam drifters.

THE PRUNIER HERRING TROPHY

Madame Simone Barnogaud-Prunier was the granddaughter of Alfred Prunier, founder of the famous Paris restaurant "Maison Prunier". She moved to London in 1934 and opened the very successful branch of the restaurant on 17th January, 1935, at 72 St James Street. Simone and her husband, Jean Barnogaud, settled down in London.

Shortly after signing the lease for her new London premises, she was invited to lunch with Charles Walter Berry, head of the well-known wine merchants, and his friend, Warner Allen, another expert on wines. After lunch, Warner Allen talked about the plight of the herring industry. He thought it was time that the attention of the public was directed to it. No one doubted that the herring, the king of the sea, had a taste all of its own and was every bit as delicate as the trout. He said that the English were eating fewer herring each year and that the fault might lie with their very abundance. The fish were very cheap and the English — being very snobbish — were unlikely to think that anything so cheap could be so good. Some of the fault could be the boniness of the fish. However, in its smoked form as a kipper it was easier to eliminate the bones and kippers had a far higher sale. He went on to explain that the British herring industry was in decline, with drifters laid up, fishermen out of work not to mention other people involved — boat builders, fish curers, etc.

Some days after this conversation, Madame Prunier had the idea of offering a trophy for an annual competition for the boat which caught the largest haul of herring with one shot, in one night, to be landed at Great Yarmouth or Lowestoft, between dates to be set by a committee. With the full approval of all authorities, she set about organising the competition. A committee of experts was convened with their headquarters at Lowestoft. Mr George Atkinson, Fishers Inspector for Lowestoft, and, later, Chairman of the Herring Allocation Board, was of considerable assistance with the provision of adjudication.

Details of the competition — to be known as the Prunier Herring Trophy — were released to the Press on 20th July, 1936. The main points of the competition were: all drifters, both steam and motor-powered, engaged in home fishing at Lowestoft and Great Yarmouth each autumn, were eligible; the boat landing the highest crannage of fresh herring in one shot — landed at Lowestoft or Great Yarmouth — would hold the trophy for one year; the cash prize was £25 and the winning crew would be invited to dine at Prunier's restaurant and spend two days sightseeing in London — all at Madame Prunier's expense. The runner-up would receive a £25 cash prize. If an English boat took first prize then a Scottish boat would take second prize or vice versa. The winner would also receive a weather vane to be fixed to the boat's fore or mizzen mast. Boats submitting claims for the trophy had to supply a copy of the docket or delivery note, certified correct by the fish salesman, endorsed by an officer of the Ministry of Agriculture and registered with the competition committee within 48 hours of the fish being landed.

THE PRUNIER HERRING TROPHY

The trophy, made from Purbeck marble, depicts a hand rising from the waves clutching a herring; it was carved by Charles Sykes, the sculptor. It was unveiled during the annual oyster and game feast, at Madame Prunier's London restaurant, on 20th September, 1936. Just over 20 years later, on 22nd November, 1958, at a short official ceremony at Great Yarmouth town hall, Madame Prunier handed the trophy to the Herring Industry Board. After such a long and close association with the herring industry, it must have been a sad day for her but the decision had been forced upon her by pressure of work. The trophy now stands with two of the weather vanes in the Maritime Museum, Sparrow's Nest, Lowestoft.

In the latter years of the competition, the skipper of the winning boat would be presented with an inscribed silver cigarette box and every crew member received a silver ash tray.

PRUNIER TROPHY WINNER, 1936

The first winner of the trophy was the steam drifter *Boy Andrew,* BF592, built in 1918 by J Lewis & Sons Ltd., Aberdeen, as H.M.D. *Sunburst.* The skipper was J Mair and their catch was 231 crans of herring. The runner-up was *Frons Olivae* from Yarmouth, with a catch of $224\frac{1}{4}$ crans.

PRUNIER TROPHY WINNER, 1937
The steam drifter *Peace Wave*, LT47, skipper D J Knights, won with a catch of 271 crans. The boat was built in 1922, at Hull, as *Telia*, H477. The runner-up was *Excel III*, from Berwick, with a catch of $249\frac{1}{2}$ crans.

PRUNIER TROPHY WINNER, 1938

The winner was the steam drifter *Hosanna,* LT167, built in 1930 by J Chambers, Oulton Broad. The skipper was W Bowles and their catch was 238 crans. The runner-up was *Allochy,* from Fraserburgh with $196\frac{3}{4}$ crans.

PRUNIER TROPHY WINNER, 1939

This is the steam drifter *Present Friends,* LT89, built in 1914 by S Richards & Co., of Lowestoft. Their winning catch was 194$\frac{1}{2}$ crans and the skipper was F Darkins. The runner-up was *Attain* from Buckie with 174$\frac{3}{4}$ crans.

PRUNIER TROPHY WINNER, 1946

During World War 2, the trophy was not awarded. When the competition resumed in 1946, the winner was the steam drifter *Romany Rose,* YH63, with 246¾ crans. The boat was built in 1924 by J Chambers of Oulton Broad; her skipper was W Rudd. The runner-up was *Tansy* from Peterhead with 229¼ crans.

PRUNIER TROPHY WINNER, 1947

The steam drifter *Patria,* LT178, built in 1916, in Holland, was the winner with a catch of 253 crans. Her skipper was G Meen. No entry was received for the runner-up prize.

PRUNIER TROPHY WINNER, 1948

The motor drifter *Dauntless Star*, LT371, is pictured here rigged as a trawler. The vessel was built in 1947 by Cochrane & Sons Ltd., of Selby and won the trophy with a catch of $267\frac{1}{4}$ crans, under skipper A Keable. The runner-up was the *Wilson Line* of Kirkcaldy with 201 crans.

PRUNIER TROPHY WINNER, 1949

This is the steam drifter *Herring Searcher,* LT276, built in 1914 by Livingstone & Cooper Ltd., of Hessle. The winning catch was 253¾ crans and the skipper was S Turrell. The runner-up was *Brene* from Fraserburgh with 231¾ crans. (See also p.84).

PRUNIER TROPHY WINNER, 1950

The steam drifter *Wydale*, YH105, was built in 1917 by J Chambers and was first registered as WY225. The skipper was A Brown and the catch $250\frac{1}{4}$ crans, from 8 miles north-east of the Smiths Knoll Buoy. She would have had 300 crans, but handed over 60 crans to the *Harry Eastick*. The runner-up was *Fumerole* from Peterhead with $237\frac{3}{4}$ crans. The *Wydale* was requisitioned in 1940 for examination service; she was returned in 1946. She was the last steam drifter to work from Great Yarmouth. She sailed to the breakers' yard in Holland towing the pleasure steamer *Cobholm*, on 29th October, 1961.

PRUNIER TROPHY WINNER, 1951

A Scottish boat this time — the motor drifter *Star of Bethlehem*, PD218, was built in 1947 by G Forbes Ltd., Peterhead. The winning catch was $303\frac{1}{4}$ crans and the skipper was G Forman. The runner-up was *Thrifty* of Lowestoft with 290 crans.

PRUNIER TROPHY WINNER, 1952

The steam drifter *Lord Hood*, LT20, was built in 1925 by Cochrane of Selby. The skipper was E Thompson and the catch was $314\frac{3}{4}$ crans. The runner-up was *Vernal* of Peterhead with $206\frac{1}{4}$ crans.

PRUNIER TROPHY WINNER, 1953

The motor drifter *Fruitful Bough,* PD417, was built in 1948 by G Forbes of Peterhead. The skipper was P Forman and their catch was a huge $323\frac{1}{2}$ crans. *Ocean Lifebuoy* of Yarmouth was the runner-up with $301\frac{1}{4}$ crans.

PRUNIER TROPHY WINNER, 1954

The motor drifter *Jessie Sinclair,* LK509, won with a catch of 272 crans. She was built in 1946, as M.F.V.1166, by W Reekie of Anstruther; her skipper was R Williamson. The runner-up was *Wilson Line* of Kirkcaldy, with 270 crans. Although she was Scottish-registered, the *Wilson Line* was English-owned, so she was eligible for the runner-up prize. The day after the competition, when she was going to sea, her crew found 8 cran of herring still in one of her lockers — had she landed all her catch, they would have won the trophy!

PRUNIER TROPHY WINNER, 1955

The motor drifter *Morning Star,* PD234, was built in 1952 by T Summers of Fraserburgh. Her winning catch was $210\frac{3}{4}$ crans and the skipper was G A Duncan. The *Silver Crest* of Lowestoft was runner-up with $208\frac{1}{2}$ crans.

THE PRUNIER TROPHY, 1955
This was the prize-giving ceremony and shows the skipper of the *Morning Star,* George Arthur Duncan, receiving the handsome trophy.

PRUNIER TROPHY WINNER, 1956

The result of the 1956 competition was a tie. The steam drifter *Silver Crest,* LT46, was a joint winner with a catch of 215 crans. Her skipper was A J Utting. She was built in 1928 by Cochrane of Selby.

PRUNIER TROPHY WINNER, 1956

This is the other joint winner, the motor drifter *Stephens*, FR156, skipper F Stephens. The boat was built in 1945 as M.F.V.1188, by J & G Forbes & Co. of Sandhaven.

PRUNIER TROPHY PRIZE-GIVING, 1956

The skippers of the two winning boats, which tied for the prize with 215 crans, are photographed here with the weather vanes which were also presented to the first prize winner annually.

PRUNIER TROPHY WINNER, 1957

The motor drifter *Silver Chord*, KY124, was a new boat built in 1957 by Alex Aitken of Anstruther. Her skipper was J Muir and her winning catch was 212⅓ crans. The runner-up was *Rosebay* from Yarmouth with 175 crans.

PRUNIER TROPHY WINNER, 1958

This is the motor drifter *St Luke,* LT156, built in 1950 by H Scarr of Hessle. The winning catch was $162\frac{3}{4}$ crans, and her skipper was E Thompson. After the 1957 competition, the rules were revised and, thereafter, there was no official runner-up.

PRUNIER TROPHY WINNER, 1959

The motor drifter *Dauntless Star*, LT367, was the winner with a catch of 189½ crans. Her skipper was G Draper. The boat was built in 1948 by Cochrane & Sons Ltd., of Selby, as the *Sunlit Waters*, LT377.

PRUNIER TROPHY WINNER, 1960

The motor drifter *Silver Harvest* was built in 1943, as M.F.V.1049 by J Morris (Gosport) Ltd., of Fareham. She won with a catch of 187 crans and her skipper was J Cardno.

PRUNIER TROPHY WINNER, 1961

Built in 1955 by Richards of Lowestoft, the *Dick Whittington,* LT61, had a winning catch of 274½ crans and her skipper was L Barrett.

PRUNIER TROPHY WINNER, 1962
Another boat built by Richards of Lowestoft, this is the *Ocean Starlight,* YH61. She was built in 1952 and won the trophy with a catch of 294⅓ crans. Her skipper was S Hewitt.

PRUNIER TROPHY WINNER, 1963

Yet another boat from Richards of Lowestoft, this one was built in 1955 and is the *Norfolk Yeoman*, LT137. Her winning catch was $186\frac{1}{2}$ crans and her skipper was R Sims.

PRUNIER TROPHY WINNER, 1964

A more recent boat from Richards of Lowestoft, this is the *Suffolk Warrior,* LT671, built in 1960. Her skipper was
E Fiske and the winning catch was $276\frac{1}{2}$ crans.

PRUNIER TROPHY WINNER, 1966

The trophy was not awarded in 1965. The following year, it was won by the motor drifter *Tea Rose,* FR346, built in 1946 by Noble & Co., of Fraserburgh. Her skipper was C Duthie and the winning catch was $128\frac{2}{3}$ crans. 1966 was the last year of the awarding of the Prunier Trophy.

THE EASTICK STORY

This section of the book is a brief history of a family which has had long associations with the fishing industry, both at Great Yarmouth and Lowestoft, — the Eastick family.

The family goes back at least five generations in the fishing industry. Mr H F Eastick was born in 1861. He was the son of Henry Eastick, a boat owner, and his grandfather had followed the same calling. He went to sea as a fisherman at an early age and gained his skipper's ticket when in his twenties, the first being his father-in-law's herring lugger *Piscator,* YH105.

When Mr H F Eastick became an owner, he stopped going to sea. In addition to the *Piscator,* he also had the sailing vessels *Heartsease, Holmesdale, Ebenezer, Ocean's Gift* and *Boy Harry.* The first steam drifter that he owned was the *Constance* which he owned jointly with his son, H J Eastick. Messrs. Beechings built the *Piscator,* which replaced the old lugger of the same name. The first engine for this new drifter was built by Messrs. Crabtree and he rapidly acquired two other drifters which were engined by Crabtrees. Thus he laid the foundations of what became a fleet. After Mr H F Eastick and his son, H J Eastick, split up, H J Eastick took over the ownership of the *Constance.* Later, Mr H F Eastick had *H.F.E.* built for his son and the *Constance* was sold. Mr H J Eastick then bought the S.D. *Berry Head* and moved his business to Gorleston.

H F Eastick had three other sons: E E Eastick, who was killed in the First World War; C V Eastick and G W Eastick. They all, in turn, worked their way up to become fishing vessel owners like their father. As well as looking after his own drifters and those of his family, Mr H F Eastick netted out other drifters over the many years he was in business. Some of these were: *Wyburn, Oburn, Jesburn, Jburn, Renascent* and *Dashing Spray.* He also managed the Grimsby-registered steam drifters *Favo* and *Cato,* which were owned by the Orient Steam Fishing Co. Ltd., Grimsby. After the autumn season was over, all the Eastick fleet would be laid up together near the ferry at Gorleston — now known as Fisherman's Quay and used by inshore line-boats.

Mr H F Eastick had the honour of showing and explaining the herring fishing to the late Prince of Wales, when he came to open the Haven Bridge on 21st October, 1930. The Prince also visited the Fish Wharf and went on board the steam drifter, *East Holme.*

MR H F EASTICK

MR E E EASTICK AND MR C V EASTICK

Mr H F Eastick passed away on 26th December, 1934, at the age of 73. Although suffering from heart trouble for eight years, he still took an active part in the fishing — he was down on the Wharf the Monday before he died. After his death, the drifters came into the ownership of his widow, Mrs Rachel Eastick; his son, H J Eastick, managed them for her. Rachel Eastick was the daughter of James Johnson, a boat owner; she was over 100-years-old when she died. Upon her death, the fleet came into the ownership of the three sons. Mr C V Eastick and his son, C H J Eastick, were the last of the family to own fishing vessels, selling their last two motor trawlers in 1975. C H J Eastick is still in the fishing business — he now runs his own fish shop in Gorleston. One other member of the family was a boat owner — Miss R S Eastick, the youngest daughter of H F Eastick. She was the registered owner of the S.D. *Refraction*.

C H J EASTICK'S FISH SHOP, ENGLANDS LANE. GORLESTON.

EASTICK FLEET LIST

Vessels Name	Port Letters & No.	Official No.	Built	Owner	Scrapped	
S.V. Piscator	YH 105	22638	1858	H F Eastick		p.69
S.V. Heartsease	YH 687	7419	1877	H F Eastick		
S.V. Holmesdale	YH 757	78258	1878	H F Eastick		p.69
S.V. Ebenezer	YH 767	78266	1878	H F Eastick		
S.V. Ocean's Gift	YH 338	108070	1897	H F Eastick		
S.V. Boy Harry	YH 370	92995	1893	H F Eastick		ps.69-70
S.D. Piscator	YH 105	111047	1899	H F Eastick		p.71
S.D. Constance	YH 326	104103	1898	H F Eastick & H J Eastick	1927	p.72
S.D. Boy Ernest	YH 752	115539	1902	H F Eastick	1936	ps.73, 80
S.D. Rhoda	YH 711	115524	1902	H F Eastick	1924	p.74
S.D. Boy Willie	YH 711	120369	1907	H F Eastick	1934	p.75
S.D. Violet May	YH 762	120361	1906	H F Eastick	1934	p.76
S.D.T. Violet & Rose	YH 757	132368	1912	H F Eastick	1934	p.77
S.D.T. Chestnut	YH 6	135079	1914	H F Eastick		p.78
S.D. Piscatorial	YH 297	128557	1910	H F Eastick		p.79
S.D. Piscatorial II	YH 762	137584	1916	H F Eastick		p.80
S.D. Copious	YH 370	135070	1914	H F Eastick		p.81
S.D. Cecil Rhodes	YH 757	96240	1891	H F Eastick	1922	p.81
S.D. Piscator	YH 105	125521	1907	H F Eastick	1936	p.80
S.D. Heather	YH 799	115549	1903	H F & E E Eastick		p.82
S.D. Heather	YH 657	137606	1917	H F Eastick	1951	p.82
S.D. Young Ernie	YH 55	144137	1924	H F Eastick		p.83
S.D.T. Herring Searcher	YH 51	135082	1914	H F Eastick	1954	p.84
S.T. Kitty	YH 250	106545	1897	H J Eastick & Others		
S.D. H.F.E.	YH 485	128537	1909	H J Eastick	1937	ps.80, 85
S.D. Harry Leonard	YH 711	137604	1917	H J Eastick	1939	p.86
M.D. Edith Constance	YH 639		1914	H J Eastick		p.86
S.D. Fancy	LT 366	122782	1906	H J Eastick		p.86
S.D. Berry Head	YH 285	111098	1901	H J Eastick	1925	p.87

S.D.T. Lydia Eva	YH 89	161639	1930	H J Eastick		ps.88-91
S.D. Young Fisherman	YH 297	136583	1914	Mrs R & H J Eastick		p.92
S.D. Wydale	YH 105	137077	1917	Mrs R & H J Eastick	1961	p.45
S.D. Harry Eastick	YH 278	144153	1917	G W Eastick	1961	p.93
S.D. Young Charlie	YH 40	140002	1920	G W & C V Eastick		p.94
S.D.T. Torbay II	YH 103	129978	1910	C V Eastick		p.95
S.D.T. Craiglea	YH 81	145544	1920	C V Eastick	1955	p.96
S.D. Lizzie West	LT 495	127400	1930	C V Eastick	1968	p.97
M.D.T. Wilson Line	YH 105	131884	1932	C V Eastick Ltd		p.98
S.D. Young Cliff	YH 126	144143	1925	C H J Eastick	1959	p.99
S.D. Merbreeze	LT 365	162956	1931	C H J Eastick		p.5
S.D. Refraction	YH 111	132186	1919	Miss R S Eastick	1954	p.100
M.T. Brave Buccaneer	LT 157	302407	1961	C V Eastick Ltd	1992	p.101
M.T. Hawkflight	A 215	302243	1961	C V Eastick Ltd	1991	p.102

EASTICK HOUSE FLAGS

H F Eastick & family on the left; H J Eastick on the right. Both flags have red and white squares.

Mr. H.F. Eastick, Mr. E.E. Eastick,
Mr. G.W. Eastick, Miss R.S. Eastick,
Mr. C.V. Eastick, Mrs. R. Eastick,
Mr. C.H.J. Eastick.

Mr. H.J. Eastick.

S.V. *HOLMESDALE*, 1895

A painting by T Swan, dated 1895, shows the *Holmesdale,* 38 tons, in the centre, with fishermen hauling a catch of herring. On the left is the S.V. *Piscator,* built in 1858 and broken up at Horsey Beach. On the right is the S.V. *Boy Harry.*

S.V. *BOY HARRY*

Another painting, this time unsigned, shows the 35 ton S.V. *Boy Harry* in full sail. Completing the list of sailing vessels owned by H F Eastick were *Heartsease, Ebenezer* and *Ocean's Gift*.

S.D. PISCATOR, c.1905

This was the first steam drifter owned by H F Eastick. The 31 ton boat was built by Beeching Bros. of Yarmouth in 1899. She was sold in Banff in December, 1906, and registered BF462; sold in Yarmouth in June, 1911 and registered YH603; sold in Scarborough in December, 1915 and registered SH188. The Scarborough Registry closed on 27th December, 1922. The boat was used as a salvage vessel at Middlesborough in May, 1927. Note the wheelhouse has been built on the foreside of the funnel.

S.D. *CONSTANCE*, c.1898

In this view, the crew of the *Constance* are lined up for the photographer. This boat was jointly owned by H F Eastick and his son H J Eastick. She was built in 1898 by Chambers & Colby of Lowestoft. When father and son split up, the son took over this boat which was sold when it was replaced by the S.D. *H.F.E.* in 1909. She was scrapped in 1927.

S.D. *BOY ERNEST*, c.1902

She was built in 1902 by Beeching Bros. Ltd. of Great Yarmouth, with 20h.p. engines by The Shields Engineering Co. Ltd., North Shields. During World War 1, she was requisitioned and, on 5th April, 1916, this boat, along with other H.M. drifters *Endurance*, LT1072, *Comrades*, LT990, *Welcome Star*, FR522, *Stateley*, BF1553, and *Pleiades*, FR489, captured a German U-boat, UB26, with their nets, 12 miles northwest of Havre. *Boy Ernest* was scrapped in 1936.

S.D. *RHODA*, c.1902

Once again, the crew line up on deck for the photographer. The *Rhoda* was built in 1902, by Gibbs Ltd., of Galmpton. She was scrapped in 1924.

S.D. *BOY WILLIE*, c.1912
Built in 1907 by Saunders Ltd., of Glampton, she was registered as YH711. She is seen here with her later registration number of FR486. She was scrapped in 1936.

S.D. *VIOLET MAY*, c.1908

This is another painting, also unsigned. The *Violet May* was built in 1906 by Saunders Ltd., of Glampton. She was
scrapped in 1934.

S.D.T. *VIOLET & ROSE*, c.1920

Steam drifter trawler *Violet & Rose* was built in 1912 by S Richards & Co. Ltd., of Lowestoft. She was scrapped in 1954. In this fine photograph, the Eastick family flag can be clearly seen on both the funnel and the mast. Her last Great Yarmouth owner was Ronald Balls.

S.D.T. *CHESTNUT*, c.1937

She was built in 1914 by A Hall & Co. Ltd. of Aberdeen, for Westmacott Ltd. of Yarmouth, but was later bought by H F Eastick. In November 1939, she was requisitioned for war service, renamed *Maida* and employed as a minesweeper. She was lost on 16th March, 1940.

S.D. *PISCATORIAL*, 1911

The photograph was taken at the Fish Wharf, Yarmouth, after the crew had rescued six men from the drifter *Montrose,* during a North Sea hurricane. The *Piscatorial* was built in 1910 by J Chambers of Lowestoft. She was sunk by a U-boat, 41 miles east-north-east of the Skerries on 23rd June, 1915.

SNOW SCENE AT THE WINTER MOORINGS, c.1930

In the centre of this wintry scene is the S.D. *Piscator,* YH105, built in 1907 by Sanders & Co., of Galmpton and scrapped in 1936. Behind her, on the left, is S.D. *Piscatorial II,* built in 1916 by S Richards & Co., of Lowestoft. She was blown up in the English Channel with the loss of one officer and nine men and is officially recorded as having disappeared off Newhaven on 29th December, 1917. To the right of the *Piscatorial II,* almost out of sight, is *H.F.E.* and to the right of the *Piscator* is *Boy Ernest.*

S.D. *COPIUS*, 1914

The photograph was taken while the *Copius* was on trials. She was built in 1914 by Fellows & Co. Ltd., Yarmouth. The boat was not to last long — she was mined and sunk with all hands, near the Corton Gap on 3rd November, 1914. Another steam drifter owned by Easticks at that time was the *Cecil Rhodes,* built in 1891 by Earles Shipbuilding Co., Ltd., of Hull, previously registered as *Rector*, GY300. She was scrapped in 1922. Unfortunately, I have no picture of her.

S.D. *HEATHER*, c.1940

This vessel was built in 1917 by S Richards & Co., of Lowestoft. She was scrapped in 1951. There had been an earlier *Heather,* YH799, built in 1903 by J Chambers of Lowestoft. She was sunk by a U-boat near the Scilly Isles on 24th April, 1917.

S.D. *YOUNG ERNIE*, c.1924

Young Ernie was built in 1924 by J Chambers of Lowestoft. It was the first Yarmouth drifter to be fitted with wireless. She was lost in a collision off the River Tyne on 18th April, 1941.

S.D.T. *HERRING SEARCHER*, c.1930

Built in 1914 by Livingstone & Cooper Ltd., of Hessle, she was sold in 1939 and registered as PD7, sold again in 1944 and registered BF19 and then in c.1947, she was registered as LT 276. She was the winner of the Prunier Trophy in 1949, but was scrapped in 1954. (See also page 44). Another boat owned by the Easticks at this time was the S.T. *Kitty*, YH250, originally registered A819. She was built in 1897 at Aberdeen and was owned by H J Eastick and others. Unfortunately, I have no picture of this boat.

S.D. *H.F.E.*, c.1921
Built in 1909 by J Chambers of Lowestoft, she was later re-registered as BK50 and was requisitioned for harbour service
in World War 2. She was returned in 1944.

S.D. *HARRY & LEONARD*, c.1921

S.D. *Harry &Leonard* is in the foreground of this picture. She was built in 1917 by S Richards & Co., of Lowestoft for H J Eastick and named after two of his sons. She was later owned by Samuel F R Spilling of Gorleston and sold to Holland for scrap in 1939. Two other vessels of the fleet were the M.D. *Edith Constance*, built in 1914 at Looe. She was sold to Grimsby and renamed *Sunbeam*, GY235. Registration was cancelled and she was wrecked on 2nd August, 1935. The other vessel was the S.D. *Fancy*, LT366, built in 1906 by J Chambers of Lowestoft. She was sold in 1920 and became a pilot cutter.

S.D. *BERRY HEAD*, c.1910

The crew are posing on the deck of the *Berry Head*, built in 1901 by J Chambers of Lowestoft. She had previously been registered as YH619 and, before that, as LT966. She was broken up in 1925.

S.D.T. *LYDIA EVA,* **c.1930**

This vessel was built in 1930 by Messrs. Hutchinson, King's Lynn Slipway Co. Ltd., She was 104ft long and 20ft 7ins wide, 12ft 6ins 41h.p. triple engine by Crabtree & Co. Ltd., and was 64 nett tons.

S.D.T. *LYDIA EVA*, September, 1931

The boat was owned by H J Eastick from 1930 to 1938. She is seen here entering Lowestoft harbour with a catch of white fish. She was sold to G Raines of the Caernarvonshire Yacht Company, who converted her for buoy maintenance work for the Air Ministry.

R.A.F. DRIFTER *WATCHMOOR*, c.1963

From 1939 until 1946, the *Lydia Eva* was requisitioned by the Royal Naval Reserve, again being employed on buoy maintenance. In 1947, she was transferred back to the Air Ministry and renamed *Watchmoor*.

S.D. *LYDIA EVA*, c.1973

In 1972, the *Watchmoor* was bought by the Maritime Trust and converted back to a steam drifter with her original name and number. She was a floating Maritime Museum, based at Great Yarmouth and was looked after by C H J Eastick. In 1978, she led the Tall Ships Race from Great Yarmouth. She then proceeded to St. Katherine's Dock, London, to join the other ships in the Historic Ships Collection. In 1986, she was moved to a new berth in the West India Dock. She is now back in East Anglia and is being restored to her former glory.

S.D. *YOUNG FISHERMAN*, c.1930

This boat was built in 1914 by J Chambers of Lowestoft and was first registered as LT141. She was requisitioned for harbour service in June, 1940, and was stranded at Oban on 29th November, 1940.

S.D. *HARRY EASTICK*, c.1960

She was built in 1917, by Beechings yard as *Ocean Rider,* but she was never registered in that name. On 20th October, 1940, she was requisitioned for harbour service and returned on 11th December, 1945. Even when she was sold to the breakers she steamed down to Aberdeen and towed the old steam tug *Ridgway* up to Yarmouth and then across the North Sea to Holland. She finally left for the breakers on 6th April, 1961.

S.D. *YOUNG CHARLIE*, c.1920

She was built as Admiralty drifter *Floodtide,* in 1920, by J Chambers of Lowestoft. She was renamed *Marjorie Grace,* LT491, before coming to Yarmouth as *Young Charlie.* On 1st June, 1926, while outward bound from Newlyn, she struck the Bucks and backed clear with water pouring into her fish hold. The Lowestoft drifters *Primevere* and *Empire Heroes* took her in tow for Newlyn. All went well until they drew level with Penzer Point. *Young Charlie* gave a heavy lurch, broke the hawser and, with barely time for the other boats to take off her crew, she sank in 18 fathoms, off Dominee Rock. She was too deep to be salvaged but some nets and gear were recovered next day.

S.D.T. *TORBAY II*, c.1938

Built in 1910, by Cochrane & Sons of Selby, she was previously registered as LT677. She was requisitioned for auxiliary patrol in 1940 and was sunk off Dover on 1st November, 1940.

S.D.T. *CRAIGLEA*, c.1950

She was built in 1920, at Hook, as H.M.D. *Rainband*. In 1920, she was registered as LH270 and, in c.1923, was renamed *Craiglea*, INS540, and finally came to Yarmouth. She was scrapped in 1955.

S.D. *LIZZIE WEST*, c.1960

The boat was built in 1930 by Herd & McKenzie of Buckie and registered as BF213, then M22, before coming to Lowestoft. She was requisitioned in 1941 and served as auxiliary patrol until she was returned in 1945. This was the last steam drifter to work from Lowestoft. She was sold to Fraserburgh in 1961 and was used as a tanning ship until being broken up in 1968.

M.D.T. *WILSON LINE*, c.1950

This vessel was 94ft long and was built in 1932 by Alex. Hall & Co. Ltd., of Aberdeen and was first registered as KY322. She was requisitioned in 1940 and used as a hospital drifter until her return in 1945. She was bought by C V Eastick, in 1954, and was converted from steam to diesel in 1959. She was re-registered as YH105 in 1962. She was sold in 1973 to Breydon Marine Ltd., Burgh Castle, Great Yarmouth. In 1975, she was sold again to Greek owners.

S.D. *YOUNG CLIFF*, c.1954

Built in 1925 by J Chambers of Lowestoft, she was originally named *Plankton*. She was requisitioned in 1941 and employed as a mine recovery vessel until her return in 1945. She was scrapped in 1959.

S.D. *REFRACTION*, c.1951

Refraction was built in 1919 by Stephens of Banff, and was registered as FR243. In 1939, she was requisitioned for duty as a mine sweeper. She returned in 1945 and was scrapped in 1954. This is the vessel that was owned by Miss R S Eastick.

M.T. *BRAVE BUCCANEER*, c.1974

This motor trawler was built in 1961 by Richards of Lowestoft, as *Boston Buccaneer,* LT157, for Boston Deep Sea Fisheries Ltd., of Lowestoft. In 1973, she was bought by C V Eastick Ltd., and renamed. She was sold in 1975 to Colne Shipping Ltd., of Lowestoft and converted to a stand-by safety vessel and renamed *Exuma.* She left for the shipbreakers on 16th January, 1992.

M.T. *HAWKFLIGHT*, c.1974

The *Hawkflight* was built by John Lewis of Aberdeen, in 1961. She was first registered as A530 but, after being bought by C V Eastick Ltd., in 1973, she was re-registered as A215. She was sold to Colne Shipping Ltd., of Lowestoft and renamed *Aruba*, LT213. She fished for a time under that number but was then converted to a stand-by vessel. She left for the shipbreakers on 8th August, 1991.

OWNERS AND SKIPPERS

From left to right these are Mr C H J Eastick, Lew George (skipper), G W Eastick, Jimmy Bush (skipper), Freddy Brown (skipper). The young man in the back row is Lew George's son-in-law.

NET STORE, WHAPLOAD ROAD, LOWESTOFT, c.1970

Mr H F Eastick, with his sons E E Eastick, G W Eastick and C V Eastick and his son C H J Eastick, all worked their boats from the Swanston Road net store. Altogether, they employed about 60 people — ransackers, beatsters and riggers. When H J Eastick split from his father and moved to Gorleston, he had a net store at the rear of Pier Plain. Two of his sons, Harry jnr and L Eastick, both worked at the store as well as sailing in the drifters. C V Eastick and his son, C H J Eastick, first had a small net store at Fisk's Opening, Gorleston, which is now Futter's betting office. When they moved their business to Lowestoft, they used the store in this picture.

LONGSHORE/PLEASURE BOAT *JOAN & DORIS*

As well as owning steam drifters, the Eastick family have owned longshore and pleasure boats. In 1914, H F Eastick owned the yacht *Kiama* of Lowestoft; he also had a motor cruiser *Brown Mouse* as well as an ex-Brixham smack *Brown Mouse* which was converted to a racing yacht. H J Eastick owned the longshore boats *Sally,* YH129, *Prosit,* YH43, and *Smiling Autumn,* YH122. Mr C V Eastick owned the yacht *Silver Line* and longshore boats *Olive Leaf,* YH253, *Janet,* YH412, and this one, the *Joan & Doris.* This was the largest boat which was worked for fishing in the winter whilst his son, C H J Eastick, worked her from Yarmouth Beach, for pleasure trips, in summer.

LONGSHORE BOAT *JANET,* c.1966

C V Eastick had this boat built at Eastick's Boat Yard, Acle, in 1965. She is a motor clinker fishing/pleasure boat, 40ft 6ins by 11ft 3ins, with 105 b.h.p. engine which drives a 3 bladed propellor through self-changing gears. It gives the boat a speed of 9 knots. It has a Jabsco engine-driven bilge pump and a whale hand bilge pump, Armstrong hydraulic steering and a Kelvin Hughes echo sounder. She is seen here at Yarmouth Beach, rigged as a pleasure boat. She was named after C H J Eastick's youngest daughter. C H J Eastick also owned the sea-going motor cruiser *Jan May* and the open boat *Janet Helene,* which he used to take out angling parties.

OTHER BOAT OWNERS

Some of the other single boat owners who cannot be mentioned in a book of their own but all played their part in the herring fishing industry from Great Yarmouth.

R Sutton owned drifters *A Rose,* YH69, *English Rose,* YH80; these were the two largest steam drifters at Great Yarmouth, being 117ft 8ins long. He also owned the *R.R.S.,* YH245, *E.E.S.,* YH740, *Fancy,* YH376, *Boy Arthur,* YH241, *Morrison,* YH78, *Girl Rhoda,* YH367, *J.S.,* YH746, and *Young Henry,* YH257.

Other owners:

E A Baker, W Balls, L Balls and Ronnie Balls, Albert A Hudson, P O Williment, C George, F H and E J Haylett, Gordon M Haylet, G Newson & Son Ltd., W J King, J Halifax, J T C Salmon, R J Rudd, John George and Jacob George, C A Webster, J Pitchers Ltd., T W Moore, R T Moore, A E Harris, C F Johnson, F J and W C Johnson, Walter Rudd, S Ward, H M Buddery, J R Plummer, W J E Green Ltd., P G Trett, W E Shreeve Ltd., J A Hodds, G S Peck, G W Green Ltd., Don Drifters Ltd., The Great Yarmouth Steam Drifters Ltd., W Brown, W H Crome (Jnr), Horatio Fenner Ltd., Westmacott Ltd., J H Fuller Ltd., Norford Suffling Ltd., S F R Spilling, G and H G Woodhouse, London and Peterhead S F Co. Ltd., Fellows & Co. Ltd., Associated Trawlers (Great Yarmouth) Ltd., R E Beazer and P G Hayhoe, Henry J Barnard & Others, G H Barnard and C E Shreeve, R N J Haylett and R C Green, A Godbolt.

The British Coast Steam Fishing Co. Ltd., had all their drifters registered in Hull but they were regarded as local vessels as they were crewed and based at Yarmouth. A similar company was R Irvin & Sons Ltd. All their vessels were registered SN (South Shields) but were crewed and based at Great Yarmouth.

ACKNOWLEDGEMENTS

I would like to record my thanks to many members of the Eastick family — past and present — for all their help with the spoken word, and for the loan of many photographs.

I would also like to thank the following for all their help:

Port of Lowestoft Research Society;
The Maritime Trust;
Lowestoft and East Suffolk Maritime Society;
Mrs C F Baldry;
Mr and Mrs J A Turner;

Gillian Jackson for editing the text;
Steve Benz for additional editing and marketing;
and many others not mentioned by name.